BACKYARD BIRDS

# Orioles

by Elizabeth Neuenfeldt

BLASTOFF! READERS

BELLWETHER MEDIA • MINNEAPOLIS, MN

**Blastoff! Readers** are carefully developed by literacy experts to build reading stamina and move students toward fluency by combining standards-based content with developmentally appropriate text.

**Level 1** provides the most support through repetition of high-frequency words, light text, predictable sentence patterns, and strong visual support.

**Level 2** offers early readers a bit more challenge through varied sentences, increased text load, and text-supportive special features.

**Level 3** advances early-fluent readers toward fluency through increased text load, less reliance on photos, advancing concepts, longer sentences, and more complex special features.

★ **Blastoff! Universe**

Reading Level

Grade **K**

Grades **1–3**

Grade **4**

This edition first published in 2022 by Bellwether Media, Inc.

No part of this publication may be reproduced in whole or in part without written permission of the publisher. For information regarding permission, write to Bellwether Media, Inc., Attention: Permissions Department, 6012 Blue Circle Drive, Minnetonka, MN 55343.

Library of Congress Cataloging-in-Publication Data

Names: Neuenfeldt, Elizabeth, author.
Title: Orioles / by Elizabeth Neuenfeldt.
Description: Minneapolis, MN : Bellwether Media, 2022. | Series: Blastoff! readers : Backyard birds | Includes bibliographical references and index. | Audience: Ages 5-8 | Audience: Grades K-1 | Summary: "Developed by literacy experts for students in kindergarten through grade three, this book introduces orioles to young readers through leveled text and related photos"– Provided by publisher.
Identifiers: LCCN 2021000678 (print) | LCCN 2021000679 (ebook) | ISBN 9781644874943 (library binding) | ISBN 9781648344022 (ebook)
Subjects: LCSH: Orioles–Juvenile literature.
Classification: LCC QL696.P2 N43 2022 (print) | LCC QL696.P2 (ebook) | DDC 598.8/74–dc23
LC record available at https://lccn.loc.gov/2021000678
LC ebook record available at https://lccn.loc.gov/2021000679

Editor: Betsy Rathburn    Designer: Andrea Schneider

Printed in the United States of America, North Mankato, MN.

# Table of Contents

Orioles are medium-sized **songbirds**. There are many kinds of orioles.

## All in the Family

**Baltimore oriole**

**hooded oriole**

**Bullock's oriole**

Males have black
and bright yellow
or orange feathers.
Females have
dull feathers.

female

male

# Living in the Trees

Orioles fly through open forests. They **perch** on high tree branches.

These birds live in trees. They build hanging nests high above the ground!

nest

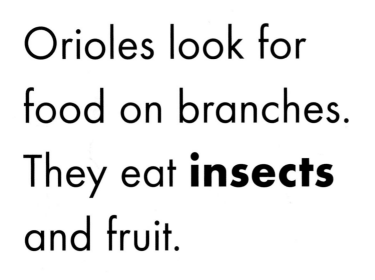

Orioles look for food on branches. They eat **insects** and fruit.

# Oriole Food

insects

fruit

Orioles live in pairs while **nesting**. Then they live alone until winter.

pair

15

Orioles form **flocks** in winter. They **migrate** to warmer places until spring.

flock

Orioles make many sounds. They often call to each other. They sing, too!

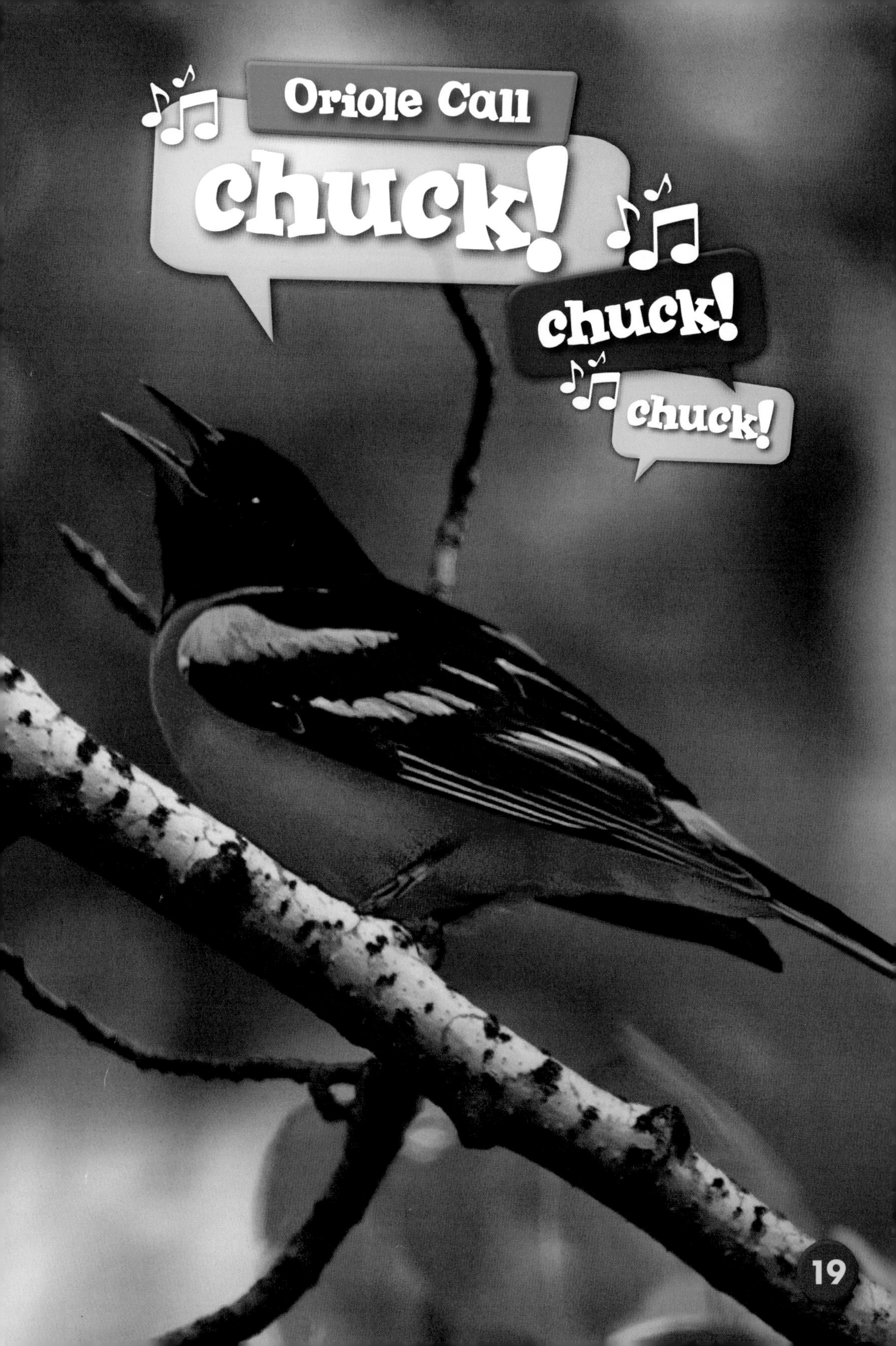
Oriole Call
chuck!
chuck!
chuck!

Orioles make
their voices heard
everywhere they go!

# Glossary

**flocks**

groups of birds

**nesting**

caring for babies

**insects**

small animals with six legs and hard outer bodies

**perch**

to sit or rest on something high above the ground

**migrate**

to travel with the seasons

**songbirds**

birds that make musical sounds

# To Learn More

## AT THE LIBRARY

Murray, Julie. *Birds*. Minneapolis, Minn.: Abdo Zoom, 2019.

Opie, David. *All the Birds in the World*. White Plains, N.Y.: Peter Pauper Press, 2020.

Raum, Elizabeth. *Birds Build Nests*. Mankato, Minn.: Amicus, 2018.

## ON THE WEB

# FACTSURFER

Factsurfer.com gives you a safe, fun way to find more information.

1. Go to www.factsurfer.com.

2. Enter "orioles" into the search box and click 🔍.

3. Select your book cover to see a list of related content.

# Index

The images in this book are reproduced through the courtesy of: Agami Photo Agency, front cover (oriole), p. 23; Dmitry Rukhlenko, front cover (background); Mike Truchon, p. 3; Danita Delimont, pp. 4-5, 22 (flock); Joel Trick, p. 5 (Baltimore oriole); MelaniWright, p. 5 (hooded oriole); Lux Blue, p. 5 (Bullock's oriole); Nina B, pp. 6-7; AGAMI Photo Agency/ Alamy, p. 7 (female); Ivan Kuzmin/ Alamy, pp. 8-9; nmgslx, p. 9 (inset); Danita Delimont/ Alamy, pp. 10-11; Roy Prendas, pp. 12-13; Luc Pouliot, p. 13 (insets); chanwangrong, p. 13 (fruit); Heather L. Hubbard, pp. 14-15; Patricia Ortiz, pp. 16-17; Michael Dante Salazar, pp. 18-19; Daniel Hebert, pp. 20-21; Triple F, p. 22 (insects); Mircea Costina, p. 22 (migrate); ThulungPhoto, p. 22 (nesting); Jay Gao, p. 22 (perch); The Wildstein, p. 22 (songbirds); Agami Photo Agency, p. 23.

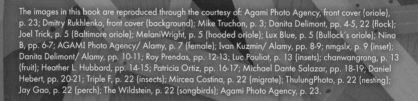